WHAT'S IN YOUR HAND?

The Game of Life

I0100138

KAREN REED

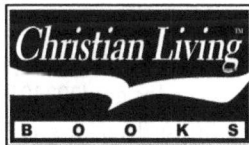

Largo, MD

Christian Living Books, Inc.
christianlivingbooks.com
We bring your dreams to fruition.

ISBN 9781562295851

Scripture quotations are taken from the New International Version®, Copyright © 1973, 1978, 1984, 2011 by Biblica, Inc.® Used by permission of Zondervan.

DISCLAIMER - This is a work of fiction inspired by my work as a coach and mentor to young women who have experienced events similar to what is described in this book. However, neither the characters, names, or events that take place in this story should in any way be understood or construed as real. Instead, they are the product of my imagination.

Library of Congress Cataloging-in-Publication Data
Names: Reed, Karen (CEO), author.
Title: What's in your hand? : the game of life / Karen Reed.
Identifiers: LCCN 2023013857 (print) | LCCN 2023013858 (ebook)
ISBN 9781562295851 (paperback) | ISBN 9781562295868 (ebook)
Subjects: LCSH: Life skills. | Teenagers--Life skills guides.
Classification: LCC HQ2037 .R43 2023 (print) | LCC HQ2037 (ebook) | DDC 646.700835--dc23/eng/20230417
LC record available at https://lccn.loc.gov/2023013857
LC ebook record available at https://lccn.loc.gov/2023013858

WHAT'S IN YOUR HAND?

CONTENTS

INTRODUCTION

As a woman who experienced many unforeseen trials in her teenage years, I have asked God, "Why me?" Now, I understand that those trials were necessary because they were part of my destiny. They were like the "No cross, no crown" of my life. These trials have refined and defined me. They were the fire that purified the gold in me. So, I no longer ask God why; rather, I give Him thanks.

As a mentor and coach, I feel it is only right to impart my wisdom to teenage girls for them to benefit from my wealth of experience having passed through that stage. Even though they probably won't relate to me 100%, still, I'm pretty sure our experiences will collide somewhere. For instance, these are some of the questions I asked that they are probably asking today:

- Why can't I be the one with a perfect family unit?

- Why can't I attend the best schools and have access to a nice car, a nice home, and nice clothes?

- What did I do wrong, God?

- Why was I dealt this hand in life?

I know these questions are not isolated to just teen girls but teen boys as well. However, I chose to focus on teen girls because I know, as an adult woman, how a teen girl's insecurities could lead them to bad or destructive behavior.

In society, we are often judged or defined by our economic status, where we live, our educational background, gender, race, outward appearance, and our family units. These societal constraints greatly impact how teen girls view themselves and how they embrace and define themselves. Teenage girls are more likely to compare themselves with others as they try to define their true identity without realizing that others are equally making comparisons about themselves. They often define beauty and success as what they see on social media, in magazines, and on TV. As a result, it can lead them to believe they are not good enough because they don't fit into having the "perfect life."

As time passes and culture changes, they are faced with many problems that previous generations never had to face, such as the false perception of social media, physical and/ or cyberbullying, and the impact of abandonment. These are just some of the problems that teenage girls face in the 21st century.

This book will focus on how God is intentional on the hand He has dealt each of us, specifically teenage girls. Regardless of what society views as a winning hand, I believe it's all in how we play the hand dealt to us by God. Make no mistake, even the person you deem with the best hand doesn't always know how to play their hand to win or have all the winning cards.

Here are a few of my favorite quotes I want to share for every teen girl reading this book.

> "Be happy with being you. Love your flaws. Own your quirks. And know that you are just as perfect as anyone else, exactly as you are." –Ariana Grande
>
> "Everything you want to be, you already are. You're simply on the path to discovering it." –Alicia Keys

One of my favorite scriptures:

> For I know the plans I have for you," declares the Lord, "plans to prosper you and not to harm you, plans to give you hope and a future. (Jeremiah 29:11)

Sometimes things don't go as we plan. Don't be disappointed; know that God has dealt each of us a hand in life, and it's not to harm us but to lead us to our destiny. My prayer is for every individual, after reading this book, to be equipped to know they are destined for greatness regardless of the hand they were dealt.

In this story I will explore the hand dealt to five single moms and their teen daughters. One night at a company's holiday party, five single moms sat at the same table to enjoy the festivities. Their destinies would become forever connected. Nicole, the most senior employee at the ABC company, was the last to arrive and takes the last chair at the table with the other four ladies. She initiates the conversation that will ultimately lead the ladies on a journey that would reveal some of the most personal challenges they each were facing. Nicole, the leader that she is, would begin describing the hand dealt to her and her daughter. I will also highlight the challenging hands dealt to the other moms and their daughters, regardless of their race, culture, social or economic backgrounds.

Each mother and daughter have been dealt challenges including social media deception, abandonment, adoption, financial access, and suicidal thoughts. They shared their journey on how they played the hand they were dealt and the strengths inside of them. Ultimately, they learn that if the dealer (God) needs to add or remove something or someone in their life, it's to make sure they reach their destiny.

CHAPTER 1

WHAT HAND WAS I GIVEN?

O N A FRIDAY NIGHT, a week before Christmas, the ABC Company was hosting their annual Christmas party. There were approximately 500 attendees, and the venue was extravagant. There was lots of food, decorations, entertainment, games, and music. I have been an employee of the ABC Company for ten years, and I've witnessed the new and innovative events that are added to the annual Christmas party.

This year I arrived a little late, and by the time I arrived, most of the tables were full. I became a little nervous because I didn't want to sit in the back of the ballroom. As I began to scan the room, I noticed two tables in the middle of the ballroom, one table with two seats remaining that was filled with mostly guys and the other table with one seat remaining with all ladies. I thought, "Let me grab this table." I quickly walked to the table and sat down.

The other four ladies were very welcoming, and I immediately thought, "Great, I think I picked the right table and this is going to be a good night." As I looked to my far right, I noticed Carmen. I met her two years ago when she began working for the organization. We worked on projects together and attended different offsites. We both made eye contact, smiled, and spoke to each other.

Divine Connections

While the food was being served, we started with a small conversation about our families and our jobs with the ABC Company. I blurted out, "Before the servers get to our table, why don't we introduce ourselves and mention one thing we are most proud of?"

All the ladies agreed. I was first.

"Hi, my name is Nicole, I work in marketing, and I have been with the ABC company for ten years. I love going to church, and I am most proud to be the mother of two kids, a young adult son in college, and a daughter Jada (16 years old), whom I adopted at three months old."

Next was Krystal, who worked in IT for seven years, and was most proud of her only daughter Tiffany (15 years old) and the fact that she has traveled to all the seven continents. Then there was Carmen; she worked as an executive assistant for two years. She was most proud of her three kids, two adult sons, her daughter Ayanna (15 years old), and her granddaughter (Ayanna's six-month-old daughter).

Tanya was next. She worked as an attorney for four years, and she was most proud of obtaining her Juris Doctor (J.D.) degree. She has twin girls and is also raising her niece Stephanie (12 years old) as her daughter since her parents passed away when she was five years old. Last was Vanessa, who has been in finance for five years, and she was most proud of working in her dream job and her daughter April (14 years old).

The timing was perfect. After Vanessa finished her introduction, the servers were at our table, and we could eat. While eating, the band was performing, and the people up front had finished their meals and began dancing.

We noticed all the excitement from the people up front, and to our surprise, the person that had their attention was none other than the CEO, Mr. Daniel Walton, AKA "Daniel," by whom everyone was so amused and astonished due to the serious stature he carries at work.

The TV monitors in the ballroom were all focused on "Daniel" doing his portrayal of Michael Jackson's moonwalk. Everyone was so surprised to see someone serious being so free and hilarious. All the women at the table were saying, "Girl, do you see this? Let's take a picture so we can remember this night." We were laughing so hard that we could barely eat our food, and the night was still young.

All the Single Ladies

After we ate, the band played "Single Ladies" by Beyonce, and of course, we ran to the floor. We all had our phones out, taking selfies and making this moment as memorable as possible. We were so hyped that it felt like we had traveled back to our high school days. You couldn't tell us anything; we knew this was the start of an unexpected bond between us single mothers. After that exciting moment, we headed back to the table for drinks to cool down because we knew this was only the first peak of the night. After we finished our drinks, we were ready for more entertainment.

Tanya looked at us and said, "Hey guys, let's go into one of the breakout rooms to see what's going on there."

We all got up and tip-toed out and went into breakout room number five. To our surprise, there were a lot of games we played in high school, and it brought back so many memories. The game that caught our attention the most was UNO, so we decided to sit down at the table and play a hand. As I dealt the cards, we established the rules.

While playing UNO, we were looking to have a momless night of fun, but somehow, we still got on the subject of parenting. It started with Tanya discussing the Christian Single Mom's Club. She mentioned the powerful support system she has with other moms and how it helps her raise her niece. One of their mantras is "God controls the hand we are dealt in our individual lives and with our families."

It was unreal because, at that moment, there was a unanimous "Yes, girl!" that came from every mom at the table.

Carmen belted out, "Isn't that ironic that we're talking about the hand we were dealt as we play a hand of UNO? Little did I know what I thought would be a playful hand of UNO would turn into an intense conversation.

While we were playing our first hand, Tanya began to talk more about the Christian Single Mom's Club. She mentioned the different topics they discuss, and she started to talk about abandonment. Immediately, I drifted off and had a flashback of my daughter Jada (16 years old), who I adopted at three months old, and how she felt abandoned by her biological family. I tried so hard to stay in tune with the game, but surprisingly, this became so emotional for me. I kept drifting in and out due to this topic being so personal. Even in trying to remain focused, my mind still went to my Jada and her struggle with abandonment. My memory of it isn't so pleasant, but I know God always prepares us for the hand He dealt.

CHAPTER 2

THE HAND OF INNER STRENGTH

IT WAS AROUND 7:00 AM, and the alarm clock was going off. I thought to myself, Nicole, it's Monday morning, and it's time to get up for work. I thought I was dreaming because it seemed like I had just laid down. I jumped out of bed and started my morning routine to get ready for work. I knocked on the bedroom door to wake up Jada, but she was already up and dressed. It was 7:45 AM. I walked downstairs to the smell of bacon. When I walked into the kitchen, the table was set with a plate of bacon, eggs, toast, fresh fruit, and orange juice. Next to my plate were flowers, balloons, and a card. This was the perfect start and surprise to my birthday.

I was elated with Jada's thoughts and creativity. I said, "Thank you," and expressed how much I love and appreciate her. She said, "Mom, I love you too!"

I looked at the clock, and it was 7:55 am, and I had not eaten my breakfast. I thought, *Why am I going to work for a half-day? I think I'm going to start my birthday early.* I called my supervisor and told her that I would take the entire day off.

She said, "That's no problem. I wondered why you were coming into work on your birthday."

A Day Together

After I hung up from her, Jada asked if she could take the day off from school since it was a light day for her. I agreed to let her stay home. We ate our breakfast, talked, and laughed about memories. Then, we decided to spend the day together, pamper ourselves, and visit the museums downtown.

After eating breakfast and spending time together, we looked at the clock, and it was 10:00 am, so we decided to get our day started. We went back upstairs and finished getting dressed. It took Jada a little longer to get ready because she wore her hair in natural styles. She decided to wear her hair in twist-outs.

I yelled upstairs to Jada, "Are you ready?"

Jada replied, "Give me 10 minutes."

Jada was trying to decide what to wear, but due to time, she chose to dress comfortably, and she put on a sweatsuit and Ugg® boots.

Our first stop was the nail salon. We both got manicures and pedicures. We were the first two clients in the shop and were by ourselves. We started talking about Jada's relationships. Jada had one close friend but wasn't into dating anyone, although she liked this guy named Damion. She seemed so wrapped up in her academics that she never pursued him.

I asked her about him, and she said, "He's not going to like me; I'm not popular, I'm not a size 5, and I don't have long, straight hair like the other girls my age."

I looked her in her eyes and told her, "You are beautiful, healthy, and intelligent; any young man can see that."

She said, "Mom, let's talk about this later; other customers are coming in."

I Never Knew

As we finished our manicures and pedicures, I thought, *I never knew this about her*. She always seemed so focused on her academics that I never realized that she didn't have a social life. Besides, she and her friend Denisha would hang out sometimes on the weekend. They would have sleepovers, go shopping, and talk on the phone.

While in the car on our way downtown to the museums, we continued our conversation. She said, "Mom, I know this is your birthday, and I don't want to make this about me, so can we talk about you?"

I insisted we continue the conversation.

She said, "You know I'm 16 and thinking about running for president of the school council, but I probably won't get elected because I'm not as smart as the other candidates."

I asked, "Where is this coming from?"

Jada blurted out, "I never fit in. It's like I have a sign on me that says, 'You're adopted, and you were abandoned by your own mom.'"

I felt pain and disappointment rise in me and tears roll down my cheeks.

I said to her, "You were adopted because I chose you. I know when you were younger, you experienced being teased by your peers who said that your mother gave you up and she didn't want you because you were too dark and ugly. I never knew this still bothered you."

Jada began crying uncontrollably. Trying to get her words out, she said, "Therapy helped some, but I still feel an emptiness. I don't know who I look like and when we go to family reunions, everyone is always talking about how my cousins look like granddad or grandma. I don't look like anyone. I'm dark-skinned with dark brown eyes, full and thick hair; and I'm a size 14. All my cousins are light-skinned and petite with shoulder-length hair."

> *You were adopted because I chose you.*

Thankfully, we arrived downtown at that moment and found a parking spot. We sat in the car and talked.

About My Life

I looked at Jada and told her, "I need to tell you about my life and why I chose to adopt you. I always wrestled with when I would tell you, but I feel like now is a perfect time. I always wanted to have two kids: a boy and a girl.

I was a young mother when I had Maurice. His father and I were best friends in high school and dated for six years. He married another woman after he left me, and I was devastated.

I dated one guy after that relationship, and we were engaged. During that time, I had three miscarriages, and after that, I decided not to try to get pregnant anymore. My fiancé at the time wanted to have kids, and when I couldn't give him a child, he left me.

For many years I suffered from depression. Until one day, I decided to get professional help. Once my outlook on life switched from negative to positive, I began to make better choices.

I knew I wanted to have a baby girl, and I wasn't going to let my circumstances stop that from happening. I reached out to an adoption agency and went through the process, and I was matched with you. There was no doubt in my mind when I saw you at 3-days old that you were my little girl. I was so excited that God blessed me with you, and I hope you know that you are my daughter, and I love you as much as if I birthed you myself."

Jada looked over at me and said, "Wow! I never knew that about you. That is what made you decide to choose me as your daughter! Mom, now that you have opened up about your life and how I became your daughter, I need to share some things with you."

Jada began to open up about crying herself to sleep at night because she would dream that her birth mother would come and pick her up from school. They would spend time together, and she would shower her with so much love and apologize for giving her up for adoption.

The Confession

She looked at me and said, "Mom, I have a confession. Please don't hate me when I tell you this. I have been secretly trying to find my birth parents. I have been searching for my birth mother online and on social media. I located her on social media and sent her a message requesting to meet her. I even sent her a recent picture of me. She wrote back to me and told me she didn't want to meet me and requested that I never contact her again. After that occurred, she closed her social media account, and I never heard from her again.

> *I'm going to make sure you get the help you need.*

Before she closed her account, I saw her profile picture and noticed we have the same physical features. This was five months ago, and I've been devastated ever since. I am so angry with myself and God because I don't understand what's wrong with me. Why doesn't she want to know me? This is my junior year of high school, and I wanted her to know me so she could be at my high school graduation next year.

"After that incident, I started sleeping with random guys and using drugs to fit in. I attended a party with Denisha two months ago because I wanted to detach from my situation and emotions and just have fun. It was a house party, and there was alcohol and drugs. I got wasted that night and slept with this guy I met at the party. Two weeks later, I took a pregnancy test because I thought I was experiencing morning sickness. The test came back negative. I was relieved because I knew I didn't want to bring a baby into the world at this stage in my life. I want to give up. I don't want to live anymore! God, why did it have to be me to go through this? Mom, why doesn't my birth mother want to know me? I don't know where to go from here. I know you love me, but my own birth mother abandoned me, and she doesn't love me."

At that moment, Jada began to cry uncontrollably. I hugged her tightly and said, "I'm sorry you had to go through this by yourself. I promise to be with you every step of the way moving forward. I'm going to make sure you get the help you need to deal with this situation. Jada,

> *I sat back in my chair, wondering, "How did I miss this?"*

you may not know this now, but you have an inner strength within, and you will make it through this season victoriously."

Jada said, "Mom, it's your birthday, and we're at the museum. Do you still want to go inside?"

I replied, "How about we stop at the bakery around the corner and get some ice cream and cupcakes?"

Jada replied, "That's a good idea."

We decided that we would seek professional help the following morning, but the remainder of the evening would be devoted to celebrating. Jada ordered my favorite cupcake, cookies and cream, with two scoops of vanilla ice cream. The staff sang "Happy Birthday" and we enjoyed the evening sitting outside while people-watching. Before heading home, we stopped by one of my favorite restaurants and ordered take-out for dinner. That night I tossed and turned, thinking about Jada's confession.

After hearing such a shocking and emotional confession, I sat back in my chair, wondering, "How did I miss this?" As parents, you can think you know what's going on with your child but at the same time be left in the dark about certain issues. Every time I hear the word abandonment, it makes me think of this moment in time because it was the first time I was able to feel my daughter's pain.

As I sat there in silence, I heard, "Nicole! Nicole! It's your turn." That's when I realized that I drifted off longer than expected. I quickly responded, "I'm sorry, you guys," because I wanted to cover up that my mind wasn't there; it was somewhere else.

CHAPTER 3

THE HAND OF ACCESS

A S I GOT BACK on track with the game, I realized that Carmen was physically present but wasn't there mentally. I noticed that Krystal had the floor and was talking about the great things that were happening in her life. I believe that it triggered Carmen based on the conversation we had at work a few weeks earlier.

Struggling

Carmen and I attended an offsite meeting the previous month to outline the company's strategic plan for the community initiatives for the following year. After the meeting, we decided to stop for lunch at a local restaurant before heading back to the office, which was something that we did each time we had an offsite meeting. While at lunch, we discussed the upcoming Thanksgiving holiday and our plans. I was planning to visit my family in California.

When I asked Carmen about her plans, she seemed a little hesitant and replied, "I'm still trying to decide." I asked her if she was going to stay local. She said, "Nicole, honestly, I would love to take my family to Disney World or travel to a private island for Thanksgiving, but I don't have the funds. I have been struggling, trying to help my daughter financially. You know she has a newborn baby girl, and her boyfriend left her when he found out she was pregnant. I'm doing everything in my power to make sure Ayanna doesn't drop out of school."

Although I couldn't relate to what she was experiencing, I was empathetic to her situation and gave her some encouraging words. I also shared some of the programs at my church and in the community that could help Ayanna financially. After sharing those resources, I asked her if I could pray for her.

She said, "Of course, you know I can use all the prayer in the world because sometimes I feel this hand I was dealt is just too much."

We prayed and finished our meal, and headed back to the office.

> *I feel this hand I was dealt is just too much.*

So, when Krystal was talking about her fabulous trip to the Bahamas for Thanksgiving and her upcoming trip to a private island for Christmas, I believe it triggered Carmen to space out mentally because she knew she wanted to do those things for her three kids and granddaughter, but she wasn't financially able to do so. I looked over at Carmen and noticed a look on her face as if she was in deep thought. As Krystal continued to talk about the great things that were happening in her life, once again, I looked over at Carmen and noticed by the look on her face that she had mentally exited the game. It was the facial expression she made when Krystal mentioned a family vacation on a private island, which was familiar to me.

A few months ago, an incident occurred where Carmen thought her daughter was missing, which was a traumatic experience for her. Carmen's family is her heart, and she realizes that they are more important than a luxury holiday trip. Months earlier, Carmen received a call from Ayanna's school, George Washington High School, about her being absent. When Carmen heard the message, she began to panic because she had dropped Ayanna off at school that morning. She immediately called Ayanna's cell phone, but it went straight to voicemail. She left a message and sent a text demanding Ayanna call her within the next 15 minutes or she would have to go to the police department and file a report.

While waiting for the text or phone call, she flashed back to Ayanna's physical characteristics and what she was wearing that morning. Ayanna has olive skin and long, straight, black hair and is a size 12. She was wearing a graphic white tee with black letters that said, "I'm beautiful," black sweatpants, black tennis shoes, colorful braided friendship bracelets, and gold, hooped earrings. Within 10 minutes, her phone rang, and it was Ayanna on the other end.

She said, "Mom, I got your message. I'm not sure why you received a voicemail from the school saying I didn't show up. My best friend's mom received the same call. Maybe it's an administrative error in the front office. Remember I told you the journalism club is going on a field trip to the local news station today?"

Carmen replied, "That's right, I totally forgot. In my mind, I thought you were going next Tuesday. Enjoy yourself, and I will see you after school."

The students arrived at the local news station and were separated into two groups of 8 students. Ayanna was happy that she was in the group with her best friend, Kierra. Kierra and Ayanna had been friends since elementary school and shared some of the same interests, one of which is their dream of becoming a news anchor. During the tour, they were introduced to the cast members and were able to hear their stories and experiences of working at a news station. Then, they toured the dressing rooms and watched the live noon-day show.

After the show, the students expressed gratitude to the cast members for making their trip memorable. Before leaving the news station, the station manager, Mr. Jones, announced his plan to partner with the journalism club to offer volunteer and internship opportunities. The students were elated! Mr. Jones told them they would get more information once the details were finalized with the school administrators.

Two Lies and a Truth

On their way back to school, they stopped for lunch at Applebee's. Ayanna, Kierra, and Tiffany sat at the same table. They were in the same group at the news station and decided to hang out together at lunch. Tiffany is more of an introvert, but she has a passion for public speaking, which is evident from her role as the event coordinator in the journalism club. She has a light skin tone with brown hazel eyes and black shoulder-length hair, and she is a size 10. She wears name-brand clothes, stiletto nails with diamonds, her hair in block braids, and flawless make-up. Ayanna remembered Tiffany from her history class and knew Tiffany was a fashionista.

Ayanna is friendly and loves making new friends. She wears a lot of tees, sweatshirts, jeans, and sweatpants; she likes being comfortable. She isn't into nails, make-up, and fancy hairstyles. Her style is more laid back, and because her hair is black, long, and straight, she often wears it in a bun or a ponytail. She isn't involved in a lot of extra-curricular activities because of her responsibilities as a mom.

Kierra is fun and outgoing; she loves to make people laugh. She isn't into a lot of materialistic things. She focuses on her academics and is a member of the National Honor Society. Her passion is singing; she enjoys singing in the school choir.

While waiting for their lunch, they started talking about everything and decided to play the game "Two Lies and a Truth." Ayanna went first:

1. I want to be an actress when I grow up.
2. I dated two guys at one time.
3. I stole food from the grocery store to feed my newborn daughter.

Both Tiffany and Kierra guessed her truth, which was Number 3.

Ayanna revealed to Kierra and Tiffany how much her mom supports her and her daughter financially because she doesn't want her to quit school. It was close to her mother's birthday, and she didn't want to ask her mom for any more money because she was planning a small getaway with her friends for her birthday weekend. After Ayanna used all her part-time checks to make ends meet for her baby, she came up short. She had to decide: steal this baby food for my baby or watch my baby cry from hunger pains. As a mom, without a second thought, she chose to steal the baby's food and feed her daughter.

Tiffany said, "I'll go next:

1. I met Oprah Winfrey in person.
2. I skipped 8th grade.
3. My mom doesn't have a lot of money; she lives off credit cards.

Ayanna said, "I think your truth is Number 2."

Kierra thought her truth was Number 1.

Wait... What?

Tiffany replied, "You are both wrong. I am not as wealthy as you think. My mom is struggling financially. She lives off credit cards and paycheck to paycheck. She is using her savings and investments to go on elaborate trips. I am not happy with my life."

Both Ayanna and Kierra looked at each other in shock and blurted out, "Wow!"

Then, they asked Tiffany, "Do you have anyone to talk to?"

She replied, "I did go to therapy, but that's a long story."

At that moment, the waitress came with the food. They all just ate their food in silence.

When they returned to school, they had 50 more minutes until the end of the school day. They sat in the room designated for the journalism club and talked. Kierra had to leave for the day, so it was just Tiffany and Ayanna who sat together and talked. They continued their conversation from the restaurant. Tiffany began to tell Ayanna about what led her to attend therapy sessions.

The Runaway

She told a story about when she ran away from home. Her mom Krystal worked long hours and never had time for her. They lived in a gated community, her mom drove a nice car, and they had the best of everything. However, she didn't have siblings, and her cousins didn't live nearby. She felt alone and didn't feel the love from her mom. Although she had all the material items and had access to the best things life could offer, there was still a void in her life. As she began to go into the details, her demeanor changed, and she had a sad look on her face.

At the age of 14, she ran away from home and stayed on the streets. It was hard for her to fit in because she was dressed nicely and well-groomed. That was a red flag for those on the streets. She stayed at the shelter at night and walked around the malls and neighborhoods during the day.

Guardian Angel

After day three, she ran into a gentleman named James who invited her to stay at his house. Due to her lack of street smarts, she agreed even though she didn't know him.

It turned out that James was ex-military and was looking out for her. She learned later that he had a daughter that favored her, but she passed away in a car accident. After day eight, he was able to convince Tiffany to return home.

He helped her see that she had a mother who loved and provided for her. He told her that even though she was angry at her mom, things would improve if they opened up and talked. Tiffany agreed with James and provided him with her mom's phone number. He spoke to Krystal and provided his address. She showed up within the hour. When James opened the door, Krystal was happy and crying at the same time. She reached out and hugged Tiffany and thanked James for contacting her.

On their drive home that evening, it was quiet. The following day, they sat down and talked. Tiffany opened up to her mom about how she wasn't happy because she always came home to an empty house, and when she was in elementary school, she would have to spend her evenings with the neighbor because of her long work hours and traveling for the job. Krystal knew immediately that an intervention was needed, so she set up an appointment with a family therapist. Over the next six months, their relationship slowly improved.

Ayanna shared with Tiffany how her mom struggles financially taking care of her, her two brothers, and her newborn daughter. Her parents divorced when she was seven years of age, and her dad died four years ago. Her mom worked retail jobs and enrolled in night school until she finally received her business degree. After that, she worked temp jobs until she landed a corporate job. Ayanna mentioned times when her mom would go to bed hungry to make sure they had food to eat. Their utilities were turned off, and the car was repossessed numerous times.

Ayanna said, "We still struggle financially, but my mom's salary at this job and

> *Krystal knew immediately that an intervention was needed.*

the resources for my daughter allow us to live comfortably, but we can't splurge."

Fifty minutes later, the bell rang. Tiffany and Ayanna said goodbye to each other and promised to stay connected. On Ayanna's ride home, she told her mom all about her day and her new friend Tiffany and her story.

After noticing how long Carmen had drifted away, I lightly tapped her on her hand and asked if she was okay. She replied in an emotional state saying, "I love my family so much," which confirmed to me that she was indeed thinking about the incident with her daughter. Obviously, certain conversations about family are triggers for her.

I noticed the sudden look on Carmen's face, like she was mentally present and engaged in Krystal's conversation about the great things that were going on in her life. Krystal started talking about her daughter Tiffany and her attending George Washington High School and being a member of the journalism club. She also talked about taking her to Jamaica for her birthday. Krystal even bragged about how perfect her relationship was with Tiffany. The last thing she mentioned was how grateful she was to provide access to the better things in life to her daughter.

All that Glitters Is Not Gold

As Krystal was talking, Carmen immediately made the connection that her daughter Ayanna was friends with Krystal's daughter Tiffany. She remembered the conversation she had with her daughter about Tiffany on their ride home a few months earlier. Since they had remained in contact with each other, Ayanna shared with her mom how Tiffany's mom was facing foreclosure on their home. So, Carmen immediately thinks that Krystal is not as wealthy as she perpetrates and that all that glitters is not gold.

Carmen looked at Krystal and said, "I know we just met, but I need you to really tell me if something is going on in your life and you're not talking about it."

Krystal replied, "I'm fine; what are you talking about? "

Carmen said, "Nobody's life is perfect; we're all going through something. So, if there is something you want to say, you can tell me from one single mom to another."

CHAPTER 4

THE HAND OF MENTAL CONSCIOUSNESS

O UT OF NOWHERE, IN the midst of Carmen and Krystal's conversation, Tanya got up from the table and walked to the other side of the room with her hand on her head. Everyone turned around and asked Tanya, "What's going on?"

Tanya replied, "Carmen, I know you're asking Krystal what's going on with her, but really, it's something going on with me, and I need to share it with someone. I'm really going through a lot with my niece."

Tanya's Story

Stephanie was five years old when she lost her parents in a car accident. It was a blur to her because she was so young. Her only memories of her parents are the pictures I shared with her. Stephanie is always quiet except when she's around me and my daughters — her two twin cousins, Ashley and Jordynn. Although they are four years apart, they are really close, and the twins are protective of Stephanie. They treat her like she is their little sister. Even though they aren't sisters, they share similar physical features. Stephanie is petite, with a caramel skin tone, dark brown eyes, and wavy black hair. When she wears her hair straight, it is halfway down her back. The twins Jordynn and Ashley are also petite, with caramel skin and dark brown eyes.

About three months ago, while getting ready for school, Ashley accidentally walked in on Stephanie in the bathroom and noticed she had a bruise on her arm. She asked Stephanie what had happened as she was headed back to her bedroom.

Stephanie replied, "Oh, that's from softball practice." The nurse looked at the injury, and nothing was broken or fractured. She instructed me to ice it and stay out of the next two games. I didn't say anything to anyone because it wasn't serious, and it's getting better."

Ashley decided not to press the issue since the bruise appeared to be getting better.

That evening after school, I decided to order the girls' favorite meal, pepperoni pizza and buffalo wings. When they got home from school, I placed the order and made a salad to go with the meal. It was Friday night, and we decided to make it a fun night, so we found a comedy flick to watch on Netflix. We all sat around, talked, ate, watched the movie, and laughed. After the movie, Stephanie and Ashley went upstairs to get ready for bed. Jordynn and I were in the kitchen cleaning up, and we noticed there was a full box of pizza leftover. That was strange because typically, on pizza night, there were never any leftovers.

Jordynn said, "It's because Stephanie didn't eat any pizza or wings; she only had something to drink."

I thought maybe it was because she had a big lunch at school. I knew Stephanie's class was celebrating Ms. Smith's last day as their English teacher. Ms. Smith planned a catered lunch for the entire class. Both Jordynn and I looked at each other and agreed that was what might have happened.

The next morning was Saturday, and the kids slept in after a busy week at school. The weekend for the Jenkins family typically included a sleepover with friends, church, errands, games, choir practice, church meetings, and working part-time jobs. However, this weekend was more chill, and we just lounged around the house. The girls were off from their part-time jobs at the mall. Stephanie's best friend couldn't spend the night, so they decided to plan a family outing. The weather was nice and sunny; it was 80 degrees outside with no rain in the forecast. Jordynn booked tickets for the Saturday evening baseball game. Everyone was excited because we had not had a family outing in a while. Instead of driving and then trying to find parking, we chose to take the subway to the game. We had a good time and even appeared on the jumbotron twice. On Sunday morning, we attended church and had a relaxing evening.

On Monday morning, I received a call from the coach of the softball team about Stephanie missing the last three softball practices. I was confused to hear this news because on Tuesdays and Thursdays, Stephanie got home at 7:00 pm, which was the same time she normally arrived home after her practice. Monday evening after work, I picked Ashley up from her part-time job. On our way home, I asked Ashley if Stephanie had mentioned to her anything about not attending softball practice.

Ashley replied, "No, mom. As a matter of fact, last week, I accidentally walked in on her in the bathroom and noticed a bruise on her arm. She told me she got hit by the ball at practice. The nurse looked at the injury, and nothing was broken or fractured. She didn't mention it to anyone because she had been icing the area, and it was getting better."

I was perplexed because the girls always told me everything. I recalled the many times Stephanie told me about a broken nail or even a headache. I said to Ashley, "You should have told me."

How Is Softball Going?

Later that evening, before dinner, I knocked on Stephanie's bedroom door and asked if I could come in. She let me into her room. I started the conversation with, "How is school?"

She replied, "School is going well. I have a lot of home-work in my history class and a quiz and essay due in my English class this week."

I then asked, "How is softball going? I know you have a game coming up this Saturday."

Stephanie had a "shocked" look on her face and paused for a moment. She said, "Softball is going well, but I decided not to play this Saturday because I haven't been feeling well. I'll let the coach know tomorrow at practice."

I was taken aback because I knew she was lying because of the phone call I received from her coach about missing the last three practices. I took a deep breath and told her about the phone call I had received. Her voice began to shake as she told me that she had stopped going to softball practice because she was no longer interested in the sport.

I responded, "Why didn't you just tell me?"

I asked, "Where have you been going on Tuesdays and Thursdays?"

Stephanie stated, "I was skipping practice and hanging out with my friend Kim in the neighborhood and would just arrive home at 7:00 pm as if I was at practice."

She asked, "Aunt Tanya, are you mad at me?"

I replied, "I'm not mad but I am disappointed. I always thought we had an open rela-tionship and if you couldn't come to me, you could always go to your cousins."

> *I'm not mad but I am disappointed.*

Stephanie replied, "I know, but I didn't want you to find out and be mad at me."

I calmly replied, "I'm not mad, but promise me, no matter how good or bad the situation is, please come to me so we can talk about it."

Stephanie was relieved and agreed she would. As I began walking out of the room, she started crying and held me tightly.

She said, "I really love you, and thank you for always having my back."

The next morning, while everyone was getting ready for work and school, Jordynn knocked on Stephanie's door, but there was no answer. She walked in after knocking a few times. She noticed Stephanie's bed was made up and thought maybe she had left early to meet Kim, who lives down the street.

Dear God

It was normal for her to walk to Kim's house, and then they would walk to the bus stop together. As she was leaving the room, she saw an envelope on the floor with the words, "Please Read Me." She opened the letter, and it was a letter from Stephanie, contemplating suicide.

> Dear God,
>
> My mom's birthday is coming up in a few days, and I don't know how to handle the feelings of not having a mom. It's so hard for me to fit in at

school. I'm being bullied because girls are always jealous of my looks. I'm tired of feeling sad and crying. I want to end the pain. I don't want to commit suicide, but this pain is too much to bear. I have a family who loves me. As my pastor repeats every Sunday, "Jeremiah 29:11: For I know the plans I have for you, declares the Lord, 'plans to prosper you and not to harm you, plans to give you hope and a future.' God, I know you have plans for me, and I want to fulfill the plans you have for me."

God, please help me!

From,

Stephanie

Jordynn yelled out to me, "Mom!"

I immediately ran out of my room; then she showed me the letter. After I read the letter, I called Stephanie's cell phone. She answered and told me she was down the street at Kim's house. Without hesitation, I jumped in the car and picked her up. When we got back home, I showed her the letter. We both burst into tears.

I pride myself on being a good mom and staying connected to my girls. I don't understand how I missed the signs, but I understood that intervention was

> *I don't understand how I missed the signs.*

needed immediately. We could not wait until the following week to meet with the therapist, so I contacted the pastor. That evening, we went to the pastor for counseling and prayer.

It Started with Teasing

During the counseling session, Stephanie opened up about feeling sad because her mom's birthday was in a few days and being bullied by a classmate who was also on the softball team. She said, "It started with her teasing me in front of her friends, then she started taking my lunch, and recently, she began hitting and pushing me because her boyfriend started paying me attention. I wrote the letter because I didn't know what to do. I didn't think anyone would find it; it must have fallen out of my backpack as I was leaving for school this morning."

The session ended with a follow-up plan for weekly family therapy sessions. Pastor Mark had the perfect referral for a family therapist because other families in the church were dealing with similar issues.

He told us, "You are not alone, family; I have had numerous families in my congregation in the last year with young children dealing with bullying and thoughts of suicide."

Before ending the session, Pastor Mark prayed over us and assured us the church would support us during this season of our lives. The girls and I thanked the pastor before heading out of the office. After the session, Stephanie was clear that she avoided self-destruction.

On our way home, everyone in the car was quiet. When we arrived home, the girls and I sat at the dining room table and prayed again. I looked at Stephanie, Jordynn, and Ashley and said with confidence and boldness, "Girls, we have a journey ahead of us, but as of today, we each have to commit to being there for each other. No more secrets." Everyone agreed to no more secrets, and we all were committed to the upcoming journey of Stephanie's breakthrough.

After pacing around the room while telling what she was experiencing in her personal life, Tanya sat down and thanked everyone for listening. She then said, "I've been wanting to release this but I didn't know when. I realized the time was now because I was about to break."

CHAPTER 5

THE HAND OF WISDOM

W HEN TANYA SAT DOWN, Vanessa reached over and placed her hand on Tanya's hand and said, "You're not alone. I just had an incident with my daughter, April. She got caught up in this whole social media scandal, and I didn't see it. Sometimes teenagers can be a little hard to deal with, especially during their high school years."

Vanessa's Story

It was April's first year of high school and as a freshman it was very frightening for her. She was anxious and excited at the same time to start high school. A week before school started, she and her best friend went shopping and purchased the latest trends in petite sizes. The weekend before, they went to the hair and nail salon. When she wore her dark-brown hair pulled up, a fresh face, and red lip gloss, it brought out her ivory skin tone and blue eyes.

The night before the first day of school, April hardly slept; she was up most of the night browsing her social media. All her friends had posted earlier in the day about how excited they were about starting high school. The short videos of them preparing for the first day as high school freshmen were hilarious.

The alarm clock went off, and it was time for April to get up. She prepared her clothes the night before, so it didn't take her long to get dressed. However, her makeup routine took a little longer. After she was ready for school, she rushed downstairs to the kitchen and ate a bowl of cereal. Before heading out to the bus stop, she yelled upstairs, "Mom, I'm leaving for school!"

I walked down and said, "Have a good day at school. I'm sure you will adjust well, and you know some of your friends from middle school will be attending the same high school."

I stood at the door until April reached the end of the street, which was her bus stop.

The first day of school went well for April. She was happy that her first period was with a girl she knew from middle school, and her lunch period was with her best friend, Taylor. After school, Taylor came over to the house, and they talked about their experiences while eating snacks. April liked most

> "I wished I had it like that."

of her classes but was a little intimidated by her honors English class because of the workload. She knew it would require more discipline and study time. Taylor was happy with her classes, but she was disappointed that she didn't know anyone in most of her classes. April reassured her that she would make new friends in no time. They talked about clubs they were interested in joining. Taylor mentioned the drama club because she had wanted to be an actress since she was a little girl. April thought it would be perfect for her, but she was thinking about trying something different, possibly the photography club.

Taylor replied, "That's different since you enjoy being outdoors and singing. I thought you would try out for a sport or audition for the choir."

April said, "I just want to try something different. Next week, I'm going to the photography club meeting to hear more about what they have to offer and determine if it's the right fit for me."

10,000 Followers

They went into the family room and started watching a movie. Taylor stated, "I have to leave in about 30 minutes to get home for dinner. Before I go, I want to show you the social media page of a girl named Michelle in my math class. She's popular and she has 10,000 followers."

All the girls were talking about it in math class. We pulled up her page and looked at the photos. She had photos of traveling to the Caribbean islands, attending concerts, and shopping at Nieman Marcus, and her closet at home was full of red bottoms and all types of designer shoes, clothes, and purses. They were both impressed with Michelle's lifestyle.

April stated, "I wished I had it like that."

Taylor replied, "Me too."

April and Taylor were infatuated with the number of followers Michelle had on social media. They knew that having a high number of followers meant you were popular and a part of the "in-crowd."

Taylor looked at the clock, and it was time for her to walk home. She lived on the next street over. April told her to call when she got home. April's phone rang five minutes later; Taylor said she had arrived home. April knew it was almost time for me to arrive home from work, so she started working on her homework so she wouldn't have much to do after dinner. When I arrived home, she told me about her first day of high school. She highlighted the workload requirements in her honors English class and how she was thinking about joining the photography club. I told her I thought joining the photography club would be a good idea. I always encouraged her to try different things.

April showed me her syllabus from her honors English class, and I said, "You are going to have to be disciplined and work on your time management skills, but you can do it."

As a mom, I was always involved in PTA meetings and had a relationship with her teachers and the school administrators. April knew being a freshman in high school would not be any different.

A week later, at lunch, Taylor and April sat together, and Taylor began talking about Michelle with the 10,000 social media followers. Taylor learned that Michelle is on another social media platform where she posts videos and a few of her videos have over 500,000 likes.

"We have to check out her videos after school," April replied.

"We will have to do that another day; I'm going to the photography club meeting this evening to find out if I want to join."

"Okay, sure, we will get together soon," replied Taylor.

After school, April walked into the classroom designated for the photography club meeting. She was the first person to arrive. The photography club president instructed her to sign her name on the sign-in sheet. A few minutes later, people started to show up. When the meeting started, about 20 people were in attendance. April liked the benefits and events and thought it would be a good fit for her, so she decided to join that evening. On her way out of the classroom, she ran into a young boy who introduced himself as James.

He said, "We're in the same honors English class."

April didn't remember seeing him in class. He told her where he sat, and she said, "That's why I haven't seen you because I sit up front and when the bell rings, I leave for my next class. It's nice to meet you." She asked him if he was joining the photography club, and he replied yes. He talked about it always being one of his passions.

April replied, "Great! Well, I have to go now. My mom just sent me a text message and she's waiting for me outside. I'll see you tomorrow in class."

When April got in the car, she told me she had joined the photography club and about the events and benefits. I was excited but stressed that she had to keep her grades up to remain in the club. When we arrived home, April started working on her homework while I prepared dinner.

Taylor sent April a text message, "Did you check out Michelle's videos?"

April replied, "Yes, girl! I can't believe she has that many likes. How is she in math class?"

Taylor responded, "You know she is outgoing. She dresses nice but it's not the brand name clothes she posts in her closet. Maybe she doesn't want to show off too much at school."

April abruptly stated, "I have to go; I'll talk with you later."

So Extra

The next day, April made sure to look for James in class. After class, she walked over to him and started small talk. They had a photography club meeting that evening and continued their conversation after the meeting. James mentioned he has a twin sister.

April asked, "What is it like having a twin sister?"

He replied, "We're really different. I'm an introvert and she's an extrovert… and so extra," he laughed. "We recently moved from down south after my parents divorced. My sister has never gotten over the divorce. Lately, she's been acting out of character. Well, I hate to cut our conversation short, but I have to catch the bus."

April replied, "Me too because my mom has to work late." They walked to the bus stop together.

When they got on the bus, James introduced April to his sister Michelle. April was shocked to learn that Michelle, with the 10,000 followers, was James' twin sister. While on the bus, Michelle and April sat together and had a conversation. Michelle asked her if she was on social media, and she began bragging about the number of followers she had.

April replied, "I don't really get on social media much because of school." April knew she only had 200 followers; she didn't want to disclose that to Michelle because she didn't want to seem weird.

Michelle said, "You have to get on social media to stay up to date with all the happenings. Let me tell you a secret; you can buy followers."

That evening when April got home, she took Michelle's advice and bought 3,000 followers and began posting pictures that she found online. She went through her phone and only posted pictures when she looked her best. She wrote captions that made it seem like she was living

> *Let me tell you a secret; you can buy followers.*

her best life. April followed Michelle, and she followed her back.

April was enamored that Michelle followed her back. She knew that she had to continue to post certain types of photos to gain more followers. She would do that when she got home each day, and her followers grew organically by 600 in one week. She became immersed in social media. She felt school wasn't enough entertainment, and social media gave her the excitement she was looking for. After spending hours on social media, it made her want to be in that world. She was getting friend requests from cheerleaders and football and basketball players. She would get DMs with invites to parties. It became an addiction. She could be whoever she wanted behind a keyboard, and no one would know.

April received an invite to a Halloween party from a girl named Sabrina, who was a freshman at a neighboring high school. She told Taylor about it and asked her if she wanted to go.

Taylor asked, "Do you know this girl?"

April replied, "We're friends on social media."

April pulled up the girl's social media page, and they viewed her photos and posts and agreed she was cool.

April told me about the party. I asked where the party was being held and who was hosting the party. She showed me Sabrina's social media page and told me she went to a neighboring school, and they were "friends" on social media. So, I agreed to let her go to the party. Taylor's mom dropped her and Taylor off at the Halloween party. When they got there, they asked for Sabrina, the person that introduced herself as Sabrina was much older. The party was full of drugs and alcohol, and they noticed guys there with guns. Everyone at the party was much older. They looked like they were seniors in high school and even college students. About 10 minutes after arriving, they heard police sirens outside, there was a raid, and everyone was arrested.

April called me, and Taylor called her mom to tell us what had happened. I had to bail her out of jail and Taylor's mom the same. We were so disappointed in them. I was so mad; I didn't say anything to her on the ride home. When we got home, I told April she was grounded, and we would talk about this the following day.

When April arrived at school the following day, James told her about Michelle. She found out Michelle, with the 10,000 followers, was outed by her best friend. Everyone in school found out Michelle was paying for followers, and the truth about her life was that she was poor. Her social media page was a way for her to deal with what was going on at home. Her mom had been a victim of domestic violence. Michelle had been teased growing up; she just wanted to be someone different.

> *She just wanted to be someone different.*

Seeing her mom not having any self-worth or identity made her feel like she needed to be someone else. This caused Michelle to have low self-esteem, and instead of accepting herself, she created a social media identity that she thought people would like and accept her for.

That evening when April arrived home from school, we sat down and had a long conversation about what had happened. I looked at her and asked, "How did this happen? I trusted you and I feel you let me down. Did I do something wrong?"

Trying to Fit In

With tears, April replied, "No, mom, it wasn't you; it was me. I got caught up in trying to fit in, and I didn't know how to stop. When I was deceiving people with my posts, I didn't see the harm. But when I was deceived and went to jail, I realized how harmful social media deception could be. Please don't be disappointed in me. I now understand that social media deception is a real thing."

I replied, "I'm just hurt right now and need some time to process what just happened."

We both agreed that we would get the help we needed to prevent this from happening again. I was mad at myself because I trusted my daughter and didn't know that social media was a big part of her life. I had to step back and look at myself as a parent and make sure I was taking enough time to pay attention to my daughter.

Vanessa looked at her other friends at the table because the game had stopped. They realized they all were going through some things. So, they decided to end the game.

After looking at the clock, they noticed that it was close to midnight. Before leaving the party, they told each other they would check in on each other and check in more on their daughters.

"We are a sister-friend circle and don't have to do things alone. We're here for one another."

CHAPTER 6

THE HAND OF DESTINY

AFTER THE NIGHT OF the party, we all left feeling a sense of sisterhood. The connections made that night could not be broken. Not to mention the "heaviness" that was released off each of our lives. Over the next few months, we checked in on each other and were more involved in our children's lives.

A few months after the Christmas party, Tanya invited all of us to a brunch hosted by the Christian Singles Mom Club at her church. We all were excited to attend and get together in person again. Although we stayed in touch via email at work and through phone conversations, it was different being in person again. The month of March focused on moms of teen girls, and the theme of the brunch was "What's in Your Hand?" There were about 25 women in attendance. When we all arrived, we hugged each other and made sure to sit at the same table. We had a lot of catching up to do, which we did while waiting for the event to start.

A Resource for Teen Girls

The speaker of the hour, Ms. Karen, began delivering her message. She talked about her profession as a community advocate for teen girls. She is a resource for teen girls facing challenging issues. She is also the CEO of Momentum Pathway, providing coaching and mentoring programs for teen girls.

She gave her testimony of being adopted at 3-days old, never finding her biological family, and her adopted parents passing away months apart in her senior year of high school. This impacted her self-esteem and worth greatly. She emphasized although society may identify her adoptive family as not being her real family because they are not blood, she is adamant in identifying them as her "real" family and will not view them differently.

Her adopted parents were older and had eleven biological kids of their own. Her most memorable recollections were of her parents saying to her, "We chose you and you are special." Although she felt the love of her parents, she always wanted to meet her biological family. She grew up as a young girl questioning who she looked and acted like. Although she was in a loving family, she felt a void that could not be filled. After both her parents passed away in her senior year of high school, that left a bigger void in her life. When she was 18 years old, she searched for her biological family. She learned that it was a closed adoption and the state laws had not changed. Unfortunately, she never learned the identity of her biological family.

As a young adult, not having parents she began looking for love and acceptance in the wrong places. She became involved in unhealthy relationships with men due to her low self-esteem. There were times she couldn't look in the mirror at herself because she didn't like herself. One of the pivotal moments in her young adult life, while at her job, unbeknownst to her she always walked with her head down. An older woman at her job brought it to her attention and began mentoring her. She shared with her an audio tape, "Self-Esteem, Self-Love, and Self-Worth." That was the beginning of her learning to value herself as a young woman. Many times, she talked about how she wanted to end her life and how she didn't feel worthy of living.

Throughout her young adult life, she credits God for placing other women in her life that mentored and coached her to embrace and love her authentic self. As a result of her embracing the hand dealt to her, she is passionate about helping teen girls successfully "play the hand" they were dealt in life at a young age.

As she was speaking, there was not a dry eye at the table. After hearing the speaker's testimony, I would like to think that every lady at the table was reminded of the experience from the night of the Christmas party. At the end of the brunch, Ms. Karen spoke about her organization and the upcoming "Teen Empowerment" event for teen girls and their parents or guardians. The event was scheduled for June, and she encouraged all the ladies to register. In addition, she offered a discount for all the ladies who registered at the brunch.

Ms. Karen's organization offered programs to help teen girls with self-esteem, self-confidence, and accepting their authentic selves. She also offered workshops and annual conferences that addressed topics such as social media awareness, bullying, and body image. There were also programs to help parents and guardians of teen girls dealing with these topics. The mission of the organization is to empower teen girls from all backgrounds by providing invaluable skills to help them become successful.

We all looked at each other and said, "My daughter could definitely benefit from this event."

Krystal chimed in and said, "This would be a good opportunity for me to attend workshops to help me relate to my daughter better."

With the discount for registering at the brunch, we all agreed that this would be beneficial for everyone.

Teen Empowerment

June came around, and it was the day of the Teen Empowerment event. When everyone arrived, it felt like a reunion due to previous interactions and stories at the Christmas party. Ayanna and Tiffany knew each other from school and being in the journalism club together. They were shocked to see each other at the same event. Not to mention Krystal did not know that she and Carmen's daughter knew each other. We all were intrigued to hear the introductions because little did we know that some of us were connected.

After the introductions, everyone began to mingle with each other. The parents embraced the young ladies, and the young ladies talked amongst themselves. Then, it was time for the event to start, and they were serving continental breakfast. We all got our plates and came back to the table.

Ms. Karen was on stage welcoming everyone to the workshop. She started playing music to get the audience energized, and all the teen girls were getting excited.

She said, "Before we get into the first activity, I would like all the teen girls to come up front and sit at the tables. The parents and guardians can stay where they are."

Next, she started with an icebreaker activity. The instructions were, "At your table, over the next 5 minutes, share what you expect to get out of this event."

Jada stated, "I want to work on my self-esteem."

Stephanie stated, "I want to learn about self-love."

Tiffany stated, "I want to learn ways to have a better relationship with my mom."

Ayanna stated, "I want to work on my self-worth."

April stated, "I want to learn how to be authentic."

After that exercise, Ms. Karen gave an overview of the agenda and provided the schedule for the breakout sessions.

The icebreaker exercise allowed the girls to feel more comfortable with each other. As they were looking over the schedule, they all agreed to attend the same breakout sessions.

There were even sessions for the adults and we got to attend some of the same sessions. The sessions were life-changing, and we felt refreshed and empowered. Krystal and Carmen attended one workshop separate from the other moms. During that workshop, Krystal looked at Carmen and said, "You knew the truth about my finances at the company party. Is that why you said that I can tell you anything from one single mom to another?"

> *You're not alone; you have a friend in me.*

Carmen answered, "Yes, as you were talking about your daughter Tiffany. I made the connection because my daughter told me about her friend named Tiffany."

Krystal looked at Carmen and said, "I've been praying for a friend I could talk to and be myself with."

Carmen replied, "You're not alone; you have a friend in me."

They hugged each other to solidify the start of a new friendship.

At the end of the event, we all shared how the different breakout sessions and resources could help us relate to our daughters and become more supportive as parents. Back at the teen girls' table, they felt a sense of empowerment after attending the breakout sessions. They felt they got what they expected and wanted to stay connected to this organization.

The girls exchanged phone numbers and social media handles. The moms and young ladies took photos and one group photo. Tanya blurted out, "Can you believe we made connections at the Christmas party, and now our daughters are making connections? This truly feels like it was meant to be."

We all nodded our heads in agreement.

Krystal suggested, "What do you all think about having a weekend mom and daughter getaway in December? I have a timeshare at a resort near the beach, and we can make it a fun two-day trip. My friend and I normally take a vacation at the same time, but she can't go this year, so we will have enough space for all the families. We can arrive Friday morning and depart Saturday night."

Vanessa chimed in, "That's a great idea! It would be like our annual reunion since we first met at the Christmas party last December."

Jada stated, "We should have a day of fun and a day where we celebrate our accomplishments."

Everyone agreed, "YES, that is perfect!!"

We were excited and encouraged each other to continue to stay positive and do the work until our mom and daughter getaway in December.

Mom and Daughter Weekend

December arrived, and it was the Friday morning of our fun two-day trip. Carmen, Krystal, Ayanna, and Tiffany rode together. They were the first to arrive and pick out their rooms. About 30 minutes later, Jada and I arrived. Tanya, Stephanie, Vanessa, and April arrived about an hour after. It was 11:00 AM, and everyone had arrived. Since we were all tired from traveling, we decided to get some rest and order pizza for lunch. The teens planned to attend a concert later that night filled with the most popular artists. Krystal had the hookup and was able to get discounted tickets. The moms planned to go to dinner and a show for their fun night.

> *Am I keeping myself from making the money I desire?*

The girls took an Uber to the concert. Jada was in charge since she was the oldest. The concert was "lit" and the girls had so much fun. They sang, danced, sweated, and loved every minute of it. It was a dream come true for the girls, especially Stephanie because it was her first concert. When the girls arrived back at their rooms, they stayed up and bonded.

The following morning, everyone lounged around preparing for the evening of testimonials. We had a chef who prepared a special lunch for us. All the ladies wore something white to symbolize new beginnings. After a late lunch, coach, so I won't have to revisit this again. Of course, I am passing the information I am learning to my daughter so that she can avoid some of the mistakes I made."

Tiffany ended with, "I am 16 years old now. I have learned that just because we were dealt the hand of access, that doesn't mean that we know how to handle it. I secretly judged others because they didn't have what I had. The truth is I had access to a luxurious lifestyle and didn't know how to handle it."

Ayanna said, "I always questioned God with how my family and I grew up. We didn't have a lot of money. There were times when our utilities were turned off, and my mom's car was repossessed. After my dad passed, we were forced to go on public assistance. I was so glad when my mom got the job at the ABC company. We can't splurge, but we are in a much better financial position."

Carmen stated that it was hard raising three kids by herself after her ex-husband passed away 4 years ago. She said, "There were times when I would go to bed hungry because I wanted my kids to eat. After doing that numerous times, I looked at my habits and asked myself, *Am I keeping myself from making the money I desire?* I continued to work hard and instill family values in my kids. I made sure we ate together as a family, and we took advantage of a lot of free events for entertainment."

She continued, "I recently decided to do a self-check and said to myself, *I didn't grow up with a lot of money and materialistic things, but am I using that to motivate myself or stay in the same mindset?* I thought if my friend Krystal could have it, so could I. I have a job that I love going to, which also pays well. I know that staying with the ABC company will result in me making good money. As a result, I have instilled in my daughter that regular self-checks can help her not let what she's going through keep her from being who she wants to be. I constantly tell her that she is a part of the generation that will break that poverty mindset without thinking that poverty is all the world has to offer. To set an example for my daughter, I decided to break that generational curse by demonstrating the power of going after the things I desired in life."

Ayanna chimed in with a smile on her face, "Yes, we did. We were always going to free plays."

Carmen stated, "After talking to Nicole, I learned about community financial resources to help my daughter and granddaughter. I'm happy to announce that I got a promotion, and I'm getting a bonus this year after being with the company for three years."

Everyone in the room cheered and congratulated Carmen.

Ayanna ended with, "I am 16 years old now, and even though we don't have access to lots of money, vacations, and the luxurious lifestyle yet, we do have access to lots of family, love, and support."

Jada and I were next. Jada began with, "I never fit in and always questioned God why my biological parents gave me up for adoption. I was hurt when I located my mom on social media, and she didn't want to meet me. Although I had a mom and family who loved me, there was still a void in my life for the yearning to know where I came from. My decisions of unhealthy relationships with boys were a result of low self-esteem. I literally detached myself from my emotions and began looking for "love" in the wrong places. If any male paid me attention, I felt accepted and wanted. The

> *I am learning to love myself more and accept my story.*

acceptance and love I thought I was receiving were really them preying on my low self-esteem. Not to mention me drinking and using drugs to escape my feelings of abandonment."

She continued, "One day, after seeing my peers going on dates with guys and me not having anyone, I knew it was time to change my mindset. I looked in the mirror and could not stand to look at myself. I didn't love myself and the person I was becoming. I wanted to be like my other friends and experience dating and having healthy relationships. I knew I needed to make a change. After attending Ms. Karen's Teen Empowerment event in June, I have been seeing a therapist. Also, I enrolled in her upcoming group coaching sessions on positive self-esteem. As a result of these changes, I am learning to love myself more and accept my story. I am partnering with Ms. Karen's organization to tell my story to other young girls experiencing abandonment."

In response to Jada's speech, I told them how I was hurt when she opened up to me about her experiences and behaviors. I said, "I felt like I let her down, and I didn't know how to be the mom she needed. After attending the Empowering Teens event, we started working with one of the counselors at the organization, and our relationship is much stronger."

I looked at Jada and said, "You are 17 now, a senior in high school. I remember when I adopted you as a newborn. You're going to be walking across the stage in a few months. I look at you now and see the inner strength within you. I hope you see it too."

Stephanie and Tanya were next. Tanya started with how devastated she was when she found out Stephanie was contemplating suicide and being bullied. She felt like a failure as a mom and that she had let her twin sister down. Her sister was Stephanie's mom, who passed away in a car accident. When she read the note of Stephanie contemplating suicide, the hurt and emotions were overwhelming. She could not fathom the thought of losing Stephanie. However, after the emergency meeting with the pastor that evening, she felt some relief. They joined support groups in the church and still attend therapy sessions.

Stephanie started with, "I am a teenager now. I didn't want to take my life, but I didn't know how to handle the bullying and the emotions of not having my mom and dad with me. The therapy and support groups are helping me. They always tell me that I'm not alone and help me identify my support system. I love my pastor and children's church, and when I attend, they always say things to make me feel valued and that they love and support me no matter what. They reinforce that I don't have to handle hard things in life by myself and that they are here to help and pray for me. My Aunt Tanya and cousins provide a loving home for me and always are in tune with my well-being. Having this support system and hearing positive statements continues to help me avoid self-destruction."

Vanessa and April followed. April started with how she felt pressured by her peers to fit in with the "in crowd" as a freshman in high school. She believed that a high number of followers on social media would gain her popularity.

She stated, "My favorite music artists always talked about the power in image in their songs. So, I felt I needed to look like I had a perfect image and lifestyle to fit in, even though it wasn't the truth. As a result, I created a false perception of who I was, and that attracted me to followers with similar lifestyles. I didn't know it would land me in jail because I was associating myself with others who also created a false perception. Now that I am 15, I recognize the deception of social media, and I embrace the wisdom I have gained from that experience."

Vanessa stated that she was grateful for the workshops and support groups she and April attended at Tanya's church. She testified, "I can see how that helped April build her self-esteem and embrace her true identity. She no longer looks for other people to validate who she is. She is now thinking about starting a campaign at her high school to bring awareness to the false perception on social media. As her mom, I make time to spend with my daughter, and our communication is improving. I also monitor what she watches on television and what she puts in her ear to avoid her going back to that place of looking for validation on social media."

Let It Go

Since it was our last night at the beautiful resort, we wanted to make it memorable. That night after the testimonials, we ended with a release of balloons to represent a new beginning. The balloons were red to symbolize excitement because we were excited to take power over our lives. The mothers and daughters solidified their new beginning with singing and dancing. We knew that this was the start of a bond that could never be broken. After the mini-celebration, we hugged and told each other how much we loved each other. Then, we got in our cars and drove off.

As we drove away from the resort, these were the things that were running through our minds. Regardless of the hand you are dealt, it's not what's in your hand but how you play the hand you were given. Once you realize that God dealt you your hand and He knows that you are capable of playing that hand, you won't compare your hand to others or view your hand as a losing hand.

You have everything you need in your hand to win in life. If the dealer (God) needs to add something or remove

something from your hand, it's to make sure you reach
your destiny.

ABOUT THE AUTHOR

Karen Reed is the CEO and founder of Momentum Pathway, LLC, which provides self-esteem and etiquette coaching to empower young women between 12 and 18 years old.

Raised by loving parents, the late Joe and Lorraine Reed, in Meherrin, VA, Karen has always had a passion for mentoring young girls—both formally and informally. She volunteered as a big sister with the Big Brothers Big Sisters of America. Karen has also served 10- to 12-year-olds in children's church. Through her trials and life experiences, she was inspired to start Momentum Pathway.

The company is dedicated to empowering young women to be successful and change the world through its unique programs.

Karen has a Bachelor of Science in Social Science from the University of Maryland Global Campus and resides in Upper Marlboro, Maryland.

Learn more at MomentumPathway.com.